The Influenza Pandemic of 1918

Claire O'Neal

Mitchell Lane
PUBLISHERS

P.O. Box 196
Hockessin, Delaware 19707
Visit us on the web: www.mitchelllane.com
Comments? email us:
mitchelllane@mitchelllane.com

Mitchell Lane PUBLISHERS

Printing   1   2   3   4   5   6   7   8   9

A Robbie Reader/Natural Disasters

The Ancient Mystery of Easter Island
The Bermuda Triangle
Bubonic Plague
Earthquake in Loma Prieta, California, 1989
The Fury of Hurricane Andrew, 1992
Hurricane Katrina, 2005
The Influenza Pandemic of 1918
The Johnstown Flood, 1889
The Lost Continent of Atlantis
Mt. Vesuvius and the Destruction of Pompeii, A.D. 79
Mudslide in La Conchita, California, 2005
Tornado Outbreak, 1985
Tsunami Disaster in Indonesia, 2004
The Volcanic Eruption on Santorini, 1650 BCE
Where Did All the Dinosaurs Go?

Library of Congress Cataloging-in-Publication Data

O'Neal, Claire.
  The influenza pandemic of 1918 / by Claire O'Neal.
    p. cm. — (A Robbie reader)
  Includes bibliographical references and index.
  ISBN 978-1-58415-569-0 (library bound)
  1. Influenza Epidemic, 1918–1919 — Juvenile literature. I. Title.
  RC150.4.O54 2008
  614.5'1809041 — dc22

                                                              2007000821

ABOUT THE AUTHOR: Claire O'Neal is a writer-turned-scientist-turned-writer. A lifelong love of reading and writing led her to study medieval literature. But upon taking a biology course in college, she was inspired to completely switch gears and study the biochemistry of disease. Her scientific research on cholera has been published in prominent journals. She lives in Delaware with her husband, their two young sons, and a fat black cat.

PHOTO CREDITS: Cover, p. 8 — Hulton Archive/Getty Images; pp. 1, 4 — Stringer/Time Life Pictures/Getty Images; p. 20 — Underwood And Underwood/Time & Life Pictures/ Getty Images; p. 6 — Otis Historical Archives/National Museum of Health & Medicine; pp. 11, 12 — Photo Researchers, Inc; p. 14 — United Kingdon Government; p. 15 — National Museum of Health & Medicine; pp. 17, 21 — Library of Congress; p. 23 — Naval Historical Center; p. 24 (top) — World Health Organization ; pp. 24 (bottom), 26 — JupiterImages.

                                                              PLB

TABLE OF CONTENTS

Words in **bold** type can be found in the glossary.

In December 1918, policemen were protecting the people of Seattle. They were also protecting themselves—from invisible influenza germs, by wearing masks. Many cities passed laws requiring people to wear masks in public during the fall and winter of 1918 when the Spanish flu was at its worst.

The Cook and the Crowded Camp

Albert Gitchell woke up early on March 11, 1918. He was a company cook at Fort Riley, in Kansas. It was his job to get up before dawn every day and make breakfast for the soldiers at the military base.

The base hadn't always been so busy. Only a few months before, thousands of young soldiers had poured into Fort Riley. The United States was in a hurry to send troops to Europe to help France, Great Britain, and the Allied (AL-eyed) Powers in the Great War, which would come to be called World War I. But Fort Riley was not ready to house so many people. It had no heat, hot water, or even toilets. These

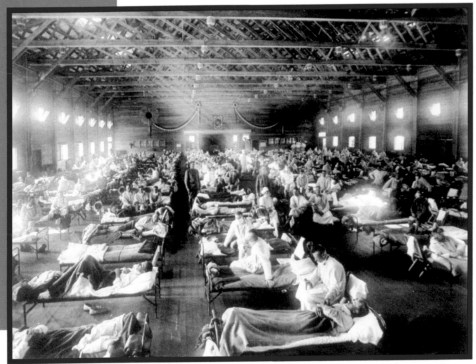

At the height of the epidemic in the fall of 1918, emergency hospitals like this one in Fort Riley were filled with victims of the Spanish flu.

conditions often made the men sick, especially through the harsh winters.

This morning, Albert would not be cooking. He had a high fever and a sore throat, and his body hurt all over. He knew he was sick enough that he should go straight to the fort's hospital.

The doctors there told Albert he had **influenza** (in-floo-EN-zuh), or the flu, and sent him to the **contagious** (kon-TAY-jus) disease ward. They knew that Albert's influenza was dangerous in a crowded place like Fort Riley, that it could easily spread and **infect** lots of people.

What they didn't know was that it already had.

By lunchtime, 107 soldiers had been admitted to the hospital with the same **symptoms** (SIMP-tums). Within two days, 522 people at Fort Riley were sick with the flu. By the end of the year, Albert Gitchell's flu had caused a **pandemic** (pan-DEH-mik), or a sickness that affects countries around the globe. The influenza pandemic of 1918, which became known as the Spanish flu, made half of the world's population sick and killed over 50 million people. In six months, it had claimed twice as many lives as the Great War, which lasted over four years.

Nurses work among canvas tents at an outdoor sick camp for flu victims in Lawrence, Massachusetts, in 1918. Some doctors believed that fresh air could help flu sufferers recover more quickly.

What Caused the Spanish Flu?

In the spring and fall of 1918, thousands of patients arrived at hospitals every day, all over the world, with the same symptoms. They had fevers and body aches and were often too weak to walk. As their flu worsened, they could catch secondary infections like pneumonia (noo-MOH-nyuh). Flu and pneumonia were a deadly combination. Pneumonia caused flu victims to cough up blood. Their skin would turn blue because their lungs couldn't get enough air. If they didn't die quickly, patients could slowly drown as their lungs filled with their own blood and fluids.

Doctors in 1918 were not strangers to the flu. The seasonal flu came every year, usually in the winter, and made a few people sick. But the

Spanish flu was not like the seasonal flu. The seasonal flu rarely kills. It is most dangerous to babies and the elderly. In contrast, most victims of the Spanish flu were healthy men and women aged 20 to 40. Also, whereas the seasonal flu typically hits the hardest in winter, the Spanish flu struck in two waves in 1918, in the spring and then again in the early fall.

At the time, many doctors thought the Spanish flu was caused by **bacteria** (bak-TEER-ee-uh). Today we know that influenza is caused by a **virus** (VY-rus). Viruses infect living **cells**, such as those that make up the human body. Viruses are very small, too small to be seen without high-powered microscopes (MY-kroh-skohps). There are many kinds of viruses that make people sick. Other viruses can infect animals, plants, and tiny bacteria.

Even today, if you get sick with a virus, there aren't many medicines available to help your body fight the infection. The best weapon people have against viruses are **immunizations** (im-yoo-nih-ZAY-shuns), or shots. Immun-izations introduce the body to pieces of the

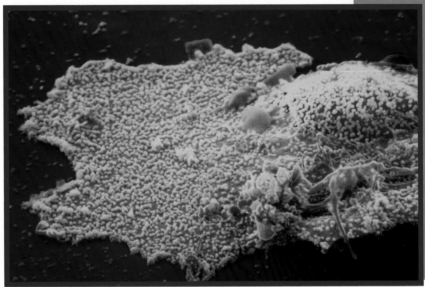

Influenza viruses (yellow spheres) invade a human cell. Once the virus enters a cell, usually in the nose, throat, or lungs, the virus takes control of the cell's command center, the nucleus (upper right, red). The cell then becomes a virus-producing machine until it dies. The viruses leave the dead cell to infect others.

virus before an infection occurs. If the real virus ever infects someone who has been immunized, that person's **immune system** recognizes and destroys the virus before he or she can get sick.

Today, flu shots are available every year. They help keep people from getting the flu. But in 1918 there were no flu shots. In almost all cases, there was nothing doctors could do to prevent or cure the disease. Either their patients got better on their own, or doctors sat helplessly and watched their patients die.

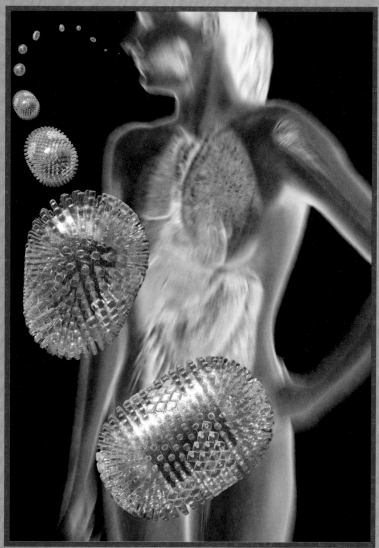

The Spanish flu was so deadly because the virus caused a "storm" in healthy immune systems. When victims breathed the influenza virus (green), virus particles entered the lungs (olive green). The immune system would recognize an intruder and send signals to the lungs. The lungs would produce fluid and extra cells to fight the intruder. For most diseases, this is a normal response. For victims of the Spanish flu, the body would not stop sending alarm signals. The lungs would produce so much fluid and cells that the victim would no longer be able to breathe.

War Spreads the Spanish Flu

When the first wave of the flu hit in the spring of 1918, it was mild and went mostly unnoticed. The Great War was going on in Europe. Thousands of young men were fighting, and dying, every day from gunfire and chemical weapons. At the time, the flu seemed like one more problem to add to an already ghastly situation.

Meanwhile, the war was helping spread the virus around the world. The young soldiers from Fort Riley were sent to Europe in crowded ships, where they passed the flu among themselves. In Europe, they fought alongside British and French soldiers in dirty, narrow ditches called trenches. There, the flu spread quickly. The Spanish flu was especially deadly to young people, like the soldiers.

The flu made a big impact on the war. It was hard to fight the war when many of the fighters were too sick to stand. Over 1 in 5 soldiers who got sick with the flu died. In Europe, 43,000 U.S. troops died not from the fighting, but from the Spanish flu. In the summer of 1918, troops on both sides caught the flu from the U.S. soldiers and passed it

Trench warfare during the Great War was dirty and exhausting. It also kept soldiers in close quarters, helping diseases to spread.

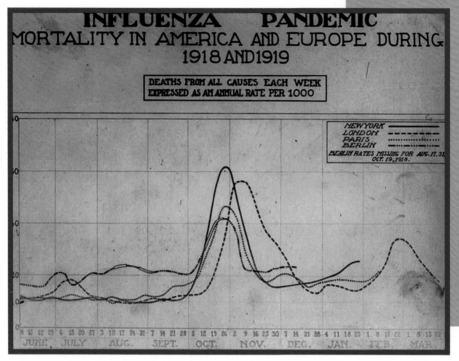

Chart showing death rates in United States and Europe from June 1918 to March 1919. By far, the most deaths occurred during the second wave of the Spanish flu in the fall of 1918.

around Europe. Many European civilians (sih-VIL-yuns), or non-military persons, caught the flu from the soldiers.

As the flu sickened and killed people all over Europe, it was also changing to become more lethal and to kill more quickly. In the fall, Germany and the Central Powers surrendered, and the victorious Allied troops were sent home. U.S. soldiers brought with them this new, deadlier form of the Spanish flu.

On August 27, U.S. Navy servicemen at the Commonwealth Pier in Boston, Massachusetts, fell ill with the new wave of flu. The flu traveled quickly to nearby Camp Devens and struck with horrifying speed. Men who were perfectly healthy in the morning would be too weak to walk by lunchtime and dead by evening.

Dr. Victor Vaughn, the Surgeon General of the Army, visited Camp Devens in September and reported that the **epidemic** "started about four weeks ago, and has developed so rapidly that . . . all ordinary work is held up till it has passed." Horrifically, Dr. Vaughn also observed

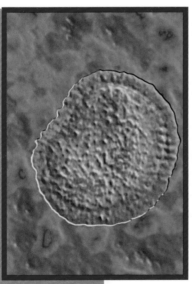

An influenza virus particle. The surface looks rough because it is studded with spiky proteins that help the virus enter human cells. Influenza viruses are very small, ranging in size between 50 and 120 nanometers in diameter (a nanometer is one-billionth of a meter).

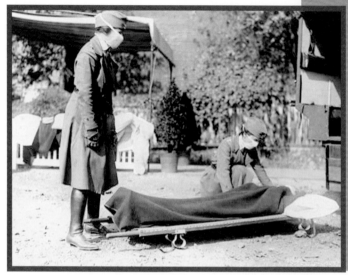

Nurses care for the very sick during the 1918 flu pandemic at the Red Cross Emergency Ambulance Station in Washington, D.C.

that each morning "the dead bodies are stacked about the morgue like cordwood." On September 5, Dr. John Hitchcock of the Massachusetts Department of Health reported that "unless precautions are taken the disease . . . will spread to the civilian population of the city."

The Spanish flu did spread to Boston, but it did not stop there. Within the next 30 days, the flu that came back from Europe would bring the entire United States to its knees.

A nurse at a fresh-air camp for flu victims fetches water on September 13, 1918. Working closely with flu patients often made nurses and doctors catch the illness themselves. A month after this photo was taken, Congress had to give the U.S. Public Health Service $1 million to hire more nurses and doctors to replace those sick or dying from the flu.

The Flu and the American Public

The second and deadliest wave of the Spanish flu began to infect people in the United States in September and October. At first, Americans took little notice, being more interested in news of the war overseas. In fact, the "Spanish flu" got its nickname because it was first announced in papers in Spain, a country not involved in the war, but one that lost millions of people to the flu in just two months.

In Philadelphia, the first flu cases were reported on September 17. City officials downplayed the seriousness of the disease. They even allowed a Liberty Bond Parade to take place on September 28 to rally support and money for the war effort. Unfortunately, the large crowds helped spread the flu. On October 3, the city finally took the same drastic measures as other cities in the country–closing schools and churches, banning public events, and requiring everyone to wear **gauze** masks over their mouths and noses. But by then, the disease had already spread throughout the city. Between September and January, over 12,000 people died of the flu in Philadelphia alone.

Minor league baseball players wear masks during a game in 1918. To prevent the spread of the flu that fall, some cities would ban baseball games and other events that attracted large crowds.

A mailman in New York wears a mask to protect himself on October 16, 1918. The flu was particularly dangerous to mailmen and bus drivers, whose jobs required them to mingle with the public.

Other city governments learned from Philadelphia's mistakes. They issued warnings and banned public events. To prevent the spread of the flu, Chicago officials advised against kissing. The New York City government made it illegal to spit in public—500 people were arrested for breaking this law. Halloween celebrations were canceled all around the country. In St. Louis, doctors convinced their city government to close schools two days after the first reported flu cases there. Sick residents were also ordered to stay at home. Many people died from the flu in St. Louis, but because of their early effort, the death rate there was half that of Philadelphia's.

That fall, the flu raged through the United States, with over 22 million people in the U.S. becoming ill. Death and dying became a part of everyday life. Little girls made up a sad new chant as they jumped rope:

> I had a little bird
> And its name was Enza
> I opened the window
> And in-flu-enza

Desperate, many people did things to keep the flu away that now seem ridiculous. Some people swore that burying flu patients in onions or feeding them raw garlic would cure them. Doctors advised their patients to drink whiskey, or to have their tonsils or teeth removed.

With so many people sick, there were shortages—not just of hospital beds, but also of doctors, nurses, and even gravediggers. Businesses had to close because workers, and

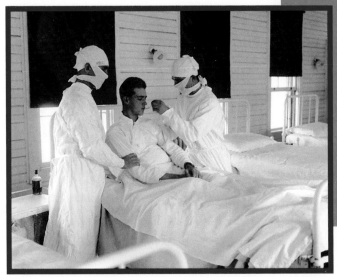

A soldier suffering from the Spanish flu in the fall of 1918 receives treatment from masked doctors at the U.S. Naval Hospital in New Orleans, Louisiana.

customers, stayed home. Everyday activities people took for granted, such as using the telephone or riding buses or trains, were halted or limited because operators were too sick to work.

The cost in lives that fall was staggering. Between 500,000 and 675,000 people in the United States died in 1918 from the Spanish flu. That is more U.S. citizens than were killed in all the wars, combined, fought from 1900 through 2000.

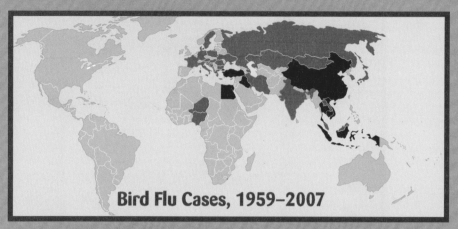

Bird Flu Cases, 1959–2007

A map of the spread of H5N1 bird flu around the world. Countries where birds have died from H5N1 are shown in red. Countries reporting human cases of H5N1 are shown in brown.

The seasonal flu strikes every year, and almost everyone, like this girl, will recover. Victims of the pandemic flu may not be so lucky. Could H5N1 be the next pandemic?

Can It Happen Again?

For a long time, no one knew what kind of flu virus had caused the terrible Spanish flu. But in 1997, scientists working in an army hospital discovered a piece of lung tissue from a U.S. soldier who had died of the Spanish flu in 1918. From the tissue, Dr. Jeffery Taubenberger (TOW-ben-bur-gur) and his research team got a sample of the 1918 flu virus.

To their surprise, they found that a protein, called **hemagglutinin** (hee-muh-GLOO-tih-nin) or HA, from the 1918 flu virus looked very much like HA from flu viruses that infect birds. The flu virus's HA acts like a key that lets the virus into cells. To HA, bird cells and human cells look different. Experts thought that the same flu virus could not infect both birds and humans.

But the scariest property of the flu virus is that it **mutates** (MYOO-tayts), or changes, all the time. Even small changes in a bird-flu virus's HA can suddenly allow the virus to infect humans. This makes a new type, or strain, of virus that no one's immune system has ever seen before. Suddenly, humans can catch it.

Usually immunization can protect people from the flu. Each year scientists at the World Health Organization (WHO) and U.S. Centers for Disease Control and Prevention (CDC) design the latest flu shot by deciding which strains of the flu are most likely to make people sick that year. Groups that are most at risk, such as the elderly, children, and people who work with children, are urged to get the shot. However, sometimes not enough flu shots are made for everyone who wants one. And because the flu shot immunizes only against flu viruses that are already known, the shot cannot protect against a brand-new flu strain.

Eighty years after the Spanish flu pandemic, flu strains in birds are again posing a serious threat to humans. The first case of bird flu in a human, from a strain called H5N1, occurred in Hong Kong in 1997. Hundreds of people were infected. To prevent an epidemic, the Chinese government killed all the chickens in Hong Kong. Despite this swift action, new forms of bird flu began appearing in Asia and Europe. Although by 2007 only about 200 cases of bird flu were reported in humans, more than half of those patients died from the disease.

Most research suggests that this new flu can be transmitted to humans only through direct contact with birds. In Egypt in early 2007, for example, three children were infected after handling dead birds. However, influenza viruses are well known for their ability to change. Experts agree that it's only a matter of time before another killer pandemic arises, and that bird flu is a likely suspect.

CHRONOLOGY

1918

March 11 Private Albert Gitchell, an army cook at Fort Riley, Kansas, is the first person diagnosed with a new strain of flu. More than 100 Fort Riley men report sick before the end of the day. The flu spreads quickly to other military bases.

Spring Infected American troops begin to spread the flu to Europe as they arrive to fight the war.

May Spain reports the flu has killed 8 million people this month. The virus becomes known to Americans as the Spanish flu.

July The Philadelphia public health department issues a warning about the flu.

August In Boston, Massachusetts, at least 60 navy sailors at Commonwealth Pier fall sick with the flu. This marks the beginning of the flu's deadly second wave, which will last through the winter.

Aug. 22 Flu cases are first reported in Brest, France, where most U.S. military personnel enter Europe.

Sept. U.S. Surgeon General Dr. Victor Vaughn visits Camp Devens, near Boston, where 63 men died in a single day from the flu.

Sept. 5 Health officials in Massachusetts recognize that the flu is becoming an epidemic. Dr. John S. Hitchcock advises that "unless precautions are taken, the disease in all probability will spread to the civilian population of the city."

Sept. 28 In Philadelphia, 200,000 people attend the parade to support the Fourth Liberty Loan Drive. A few days later, so many people become sick that the city declares that the flu is epidemic there. Public gathering places, such as theaters, churches, and schools, are closed until further notice.

Oct. Russians start to get the flu after Allied soldiers help Russian groups fight communists in the city of Archangel.

Oct. 2 In Boston, 202 people have died. The city cancels liberty parades and other public events.

Oct. 3 By this time the flu has arrived in Seattle, with 700 people sick and one person dead.

Oct. 6 In one day, 289 Philadelphians die from the flu.

Oct. 30 Washington state passes a law that requires people to wear gauze masks in public.

Oct. 31 Halloween events nationwide are canceled.
In one month, 195,000 people in the U.S. die of Spanish flu. In New York, 851 people die in a single day. In Chicago, the crime rate drops 43 percent. Authorities think this is because criminals must have stayed home in bed with the flu.

Nov. 11 Armistice Day is declared as World War I ends. Celebrations bring crowds together, and flu cases increase again. One month after a celebration in San Francisco, 5,000 new cases of the flu are reported.

1919

Jan. Seattle reopens its schools.

March For the first time since the outbreak began, no new deaths from influenza are reported in Seattle. As quickly as it appeared, the flu silently vanishes around the country.

1927   Researchers estimate that the Spanish flu killed 21.5 million people worldwide.

1940s   The U.S. military develops and approves the first flu vaccine for use during World War II. The virus is grown in chicken eggs and then inactivated, a procedure that is still used to produce most of the vaccine supply today.

1991   Researchers re-estimate, saying that over 30 million people died from the Spanish flu.

1997   Dr. Jeffery Taubenberger and his lab at the Armed Forces Institute of Pathology extract a sample of Spanish flu virus from a 79-year-old piece of lung tissue, which came from a soldier who died of the flu.

2002   Using records from countries in Asia and Africa that weren't included in previous estimates, the *Bulletin of the History of Medicine* estimates that a staggering 50 to 100 million people worldwide died from the Spanish flu.

2005   The Taubenberger lab uses genes from a flu virus sample to re-create actual Spanish flu virus for study in mice. Some researchers criticize him, saying that the virus he re-created could become a bioterrorism weapon in the wrong hands. Researchers note that the H5N1 virus that causes bird flu is a lot like the virus H1N1 that caused the 1918 flu pandemic.

2007   Dr. Kirsty Duncan and a team of researchers recover pieces of the 1918 virus from multiple organs of its victims, proving that the flu affected more of the body than just the lungs.

FIND OUT MORE

Books

Aronson, Virginia. *The Influenza Pandemic of 1918.* New York: Chelsea House Publications, 2000.

Laskey, Elizabeth. *Flu.* Chicago: Heinemann Library, 2003.

Works Consulted

"1918 Spanish Flu Timeline." *Twoop Timelines.* http://www.twoop.com/medicine/archives/2005/10/1918_spanish_flu.html

The 1918–1919 Pandemic of Influenza: The Urban Impact in the Western World. Edited by Fred R. van Hartesveldt. Lewiston, NY: The Edwin Mellen Press, 1992.

Bakalar, Nicholas. "How (and How Not) to Battle Flu: A Tale of 23 Cities." *New York Times*, April 17, 2007. http://www.nytimes.com/2007/04/17/health/17flu.html?ex=1179028800&en=66e80529f91ee164&ei=5070

Billings, Molly. "The 1918 Influenza Pandemic." http://virus.stanford.edu/uda/

Board on Global Health. *The Threat of Pandemic Influenza: Are We Ready?* Workshop Summary. Washington, D.C.: The National Academies Press, 2005.

Byerly, Carol R. *Fever of War: The Influenza Epidemic in the U.S. Army During World War I.* New York: New York University Press, 2005.

FIND OUT MORE

"Cumulative Number of Confirmed Human Cases of Avian Influenza A/(H5N1) Reported to WHO." The World Health Organization, April 11, 2007. http://www.who.int/csr/disease/avian_influenza/country/cases_table_2007_04_11/en/index.html

Davies, Pete. *The Devil's Flu.* New York: Henry Holt and Company, 2000.

DeNoon, Daniel J. "Timeline: Avian and Pandemic Influenza." *FOX News.* November 2, 2005. http://www.foxnews.com/story/0,2933,174321,00.html

Ewald, Paul. *Evolution of Infectious Disease.* Oxford: Oxford University Press, 1994.

Goodson, Lori. "Pandemic." *Manhattan Mercury,* March 1, 1998. http://members.cox.net/~tjohnston7/ww1hist/flu.html

Handwerk, Brian. " 'Bird Flu' Similar to Deadly 1918 Flu, Gene Study Finds." *National Geographic News,* October 5, 2005. http://news.nationalgeographic.com/news/2005/10/1005_051005_bird_flu.html

Hoeling, A. A. *The Great Epidemic.* Boston: Little, Brown and Company, 1961.

"Invasion from the Steppes." *Time.* Monday, February 20, 1978. http://www.time.com/time/magazine/article/0,9171,948035,00.html

Kolata, Gina. "Hazard in Hunt for New Flu: Looking for Bugs in All the Wrong Places." *New York Times*, November 8, 2005.

Korsman, Stephen. "Vaccines." *Influenza Report.* Bernd Sebastian Kamps, Christian Hoffmann and Wolfgang Preiser (Editors). http://www.influenzareport.com/ir/vaccines.htm

"A Letter from Camp Devens," September 29, 1918. *American Experience, Influenza 1918.* PBS. http://www.pbs.org/wgbh/amex/influenza/sfeature/devens.html

Stevens, James, Adam L. Corper, Christopher F. Basler, Jeffery K. Taubenberger, Peter Palese, and Ian A. Wilson. "Structure of the Uncleaved Human H1 Hemagglutinin from the Extinct 1918 Influenza Virus." *Science,* March 19, 2004.

Stevens, James, Ola Blixt, Terrence M. Tumpey, Jeffery K. Taubenberger, James C. Paulson, and Ian A. Wilson. "Structure and Receptor Specificity of the Hemagglutinin from an H5N1 Influenza Virus." *Science,* April 21, 2006.

Taubenberger, Jeffery, Ann H. Reid, Amy E. Krafft, Karen E. Bijwaard, Thomas G. Fanning. "Initial Genetic Characterization of the 1918 'Spanish' Influenza Virus." *Science,* March 21, 1997.

"WEB FOCUS: Avian Flu Timeline." *Nature.* http://www.nature.com/nature/focus/avianflu/timeline.html

On the Internet

Centers for Disease Control and Prevention—Pandemic Flu http://pandemicflu.gov/

KidsHealth for Kids http://kidshealth.org/kid/ill_injure/sick/flu.html

PBS—"The American Experience: Influenza 1918" http://www.pbs.org/wgbh/amex/influenza/

Turner, Natasha, ND. "Should You Get the Flu Shot?" April 2007, http://www.truestarhealth.com/members/cm_archives07ML4P1A10.html

World Health Organization—Influenza page http://www.who.int/topics/influenza/en/

GLOSSARY

bacteria (bak-TEER-ee-uh)—A one-celled, living creature that sometimes causes disease.

cell (SEL)—A small unit of a living creature.

contagious (kon-TAY-jus)—Able to spread easily from one person to another.

epidemic (eh-pih-DEH-mik)—A disease that infects many people within a region or community at the same time.

gauze (GAWZ)—A thin fabric often used for bandages.

hemagglutinin (hee-muh-GLOO-tih-nin)—A virus-made protein that helps the flu virus gain access to blood cells.

immune (ih-MYOON) **system**—The defense system in animal bodies that protects against disease.

immunization (im-yoo-nih-ZAY-shun)—A shot that contains pieces of a virus that will not cause infection but will help the body fight whole viruses.

influenza (in-floo-EN-zuh)—A contagious disease caused by a virus with symptoms such as fever, severe aches and pains, a dry cough, a sore throat, and overall weakness.

infect—Attack and make sick.

mutate (MYOO-tayt)—Change.

pandemic (pan-DEH-mik)—A disease that occurs over a very wide area, such as several countries, and infects an extremely high percentage of people there at the same time.

symptom (SIMP-tum)—A sign that a disease is present.

virus (VY-rus)—A very small molecule that grows and multiplies inside living cells, causing disease.

INDEX